Sympathet

Sympathetic Magic

Brian Fewster

Poor Tom's Press

Some of the poems printed here have been published in *Poetry Review, Staple, Envoi, English in Education, Limestone Landscape, Nottingham Evening Post, Poetry Nottingham, Poetry Monthly, A Chide's Alphabet, The Frogmore Papers, The Journal, The Interpreter's House.*

Thanks to them – and to Karin Koller, David Bircumshaw, Bernice Lewis and Nick Swingler for help and advice.

Published by Poor Tom's Press
89a Winchester Avenue
Leicester LE3 1AY.

Set in Bookman Old Style.
Printed and bound by Lightning Source UK Ltd
6 Precedent Drive
Rooksley
Milton Keynes MK13 8PR.

British Cataloguing-in-Publication Data
A catalogue record for this book is available
from the British Library.

ISBN 978-0-9543-3715-5

Cover picture: *Mask from Torres Strait, Australia, 1877* (1884.114.3), reproduced by permission of the Pitt Rivers Museum, University of Oxford.

Contents

One Step at a Time 7
Walking on the Glacier 8
Ice Age 9
Refugee 10
On Ingleborough 11
Moorland 12
Fatstock 13
Infestation 14
Skin Tender 15
Bindweed 16
Time, Please 17
The Parcel 18
Fragments Overheard at Northampton Asylum 19
Three Poems for Jane
  Magnum Opus 20
  Heart-Lung Transplant 22
  What's Left 24
Unfinished Business 26
Mother and Son 27
Come Back 28
Polyp 30
Lares 32
The Dark Lady's Reply 33
Winding Up 34
Statues 35
Unplugged 36
No Through Way 37
Town Squirrel 38
Bat 39
Distant Flight 40
Flightpaths 41
Encounter 42
Blackbird 43
Resistance 44
Pussycat 45
Anti-Sestina 46
Art 48
Productivity 50

The Rules 51
Kind Ghost 52
To a Piece of Software 53
Two Voices 54
Sweet Charity 55
Sympathetic Magic 56
Not Marble... 58
The Poet Bequeaths his Germs 59
Mask 60
Talents 61
All Present and Correct 62
Air and Earth 64
Snap 65
Sodden and Unkind 66
Encouragement to a Foot Soldier 67
Treadmill 68
Christmas Turkeys 69
The Death of the Ogre 70
My 9:11 71
Autumn Room 72
Presence 73
Border 74
In Memory of John Thomas 76
Take 2 77
Alternatives 78
Sun 79
Genes 79
The Real World 79
Fairy Tale 80
The Bad Fairy at the Christening 81
Optimist 82
In Camera 83
Advice to Poets 84
A Poem Prays for Survival 85
Author! Author! 86
Letter to a Crowded House 87
Summering In 88
Epithalamion 89
How Soon Has Time 90
Boy on a Landing 91

One Step at a Time

You had no hall. Behind the door
of your front room the letters lay
like drifts of decomposing leaves.
You stepped across them twice a day.

You stepped across them twice a day
while junk promotion, final bill
and family tidings cried at you.
The cries ascended small and shrill.

The cries ascended small and shrill
of courts, of creditors to pay.
With steadfastness like Saint Jerome
you turned your conscious mind away.

You turned your conscious mind away,
but some disturbance stirred there still.
A breasting wave blocked out your light.
A shadow paralysed your will.

A shadow paralysed your will.
You turned your conscious mind away.
The cries ascended small and shrill.
You stepped across them twice a day.

Walking on the Glacier

Keep to what's level, they said, avoid the slope
that funnels to the centre.

Seeing you on the ice, we waved and shouted
but you kept steady in the wrong direction,
ignored our urgency
for fear of panic.

(Your voice is brittle down the telephone.)

Skirting it now
I test the slope and traction,
am conscious of the treacherous sideways pull,
hear the insistent call of the ice funnel.

Ice Age

I dreamt the earth was under ice again
and we were left a continent apart
with glaciers between us. Where and when
our ways had forked and what was at the heart
of that divide were undisclosed. The past
was out of reach and time had blanked your track.
I dreamt I told a woman of my quest
to cross the frozen peaks and bring you back.

I'm friends with my four husbands, she replied.
I held her warmth as we lay side by side.

Refugee

Out of the harvest valley
wrapped in a cloak of grass
travelled unseasonally,
came to the mountain pass

slung with a box of embers,
bow with a broken string;
came as late September's
snow-wind began to sing;

came as a late arriver
just when the weather turned,
fugitive last survivor,
village behind him burned;

knelt in his need of sleeping,
propped on the rock his bow,
gave himself to the creeping
late Neolithic snow.

Snow took the gift and sank it
under inhuman cold,
inside an ice blanket
washed and powdered and rolled,

made deaf to all migrations
of settlement or war
a hundred generations,
and then a hundred more,

till body's resurrection,
when unangelic eyes
with scholarly selection
begin to analyse

in scraps of bark and leather
about the shrivelled flesh,
heaven and hell together
inseparably fresh.

On Ingleborough

You've climbed so far – clambering left and right
up the stone pathway like a spiral stair –
no middle distances remain in sight.
One more steep ledge and suddenly you're there.
The wind, unhindered by the mountain's height,
streams past and scarcely interrupts its pace
across the empty acres of the air
to lash this frozen gauntlet in your face.

Close to the clouds, above the curlew's call,
the skyline tightens like a poacher's snare.
On every side there's unrestricted light.
The moss beneath your feet's resilient.
You've time to rest against the lookout wall
before you start the difficult descent.

Moorland

A lean, stripped country:
bony spine and shoulderblades
stir beneath fell-boots.

The grazed valley side
is like a mildewed saddle
infested with lice.

Dirty grey boulders
huddle together up the hill
camouflaged as sheep.

In the ancient barn
past lives try to coalesce
around ancient tools.

Clouds disintegrate,
sliding over the hill's edge
into the sky's lake.

Fatstock

Heavy men hunched where the halfdoors swing
slap woolly rumps and make them trot
round like acts in a circus ring
showing the punters what they've got.

Feed, field, fodder - it's all solid matter,
everything's weighed in scales of brass.
Farmers nod to the auctioneer's patter:
time is money and flesh is grass.

Strong rams, fat lambs, sheep and cattle
process through to a huckster's clamour.
Pounds are a cranked-out gatling rattle.
Fate's as cold as the crack of a hammer.

Infestation

Some days are so besieged with wings
I've scarcely taken breath
unbrushed with subtle shadowings
of sex and self and death.

They flicker round calescent lights,
obscure the room with raids
of kamikaze appetites
and weight the unclean shades.

It's here I come to dust my selves –
clay-footed, florid-faced
stiff statuettes displayed on shelves
in antiquated taste.

And where the self itself is sham,
there isn't space that's free
of *who* and *how* and *here I am*,
manipulating me.

Some days are so besieged with wings
I've scarcely taken breath
unbrushed with subtle shadowings
of sex and self and death.

Skin Tender

From textual analyses of letters,
from synchronicities of casual meeting,
from fantasies of failure and fulfilment,
the irrevocable move that cancels friendship
and turns its ambiguities of promise
to something more intense, more coarse and subtle,
exclusive and demanding and defining,

by education in hypocrisy,
by studied carelessness of public speech,
elaborate subterfuge of assignation
and lack of unconditional intimacy
(telephone conversations in the bedroom
evading reference to the scented cave,
the electricity of halflit skin)

to a depreciating currency
of tenderness becoming automatic,
of bridling at unquestioned expectations
and improvised routines that grow familiar
and risks without proportionate repayment
and trials that outnumber satisfactions
and sentence passed: "Of course we must stay *friends*".

Bindweed

after DHL

The creeper-choked embankment wall that looms,
most fitting for a dream or fairy tale,
twenty feet high at the bottom of the garden
this summer's burning with convolvulus
in great white blotches like magnesium flares
that creep across the gap and through next door's
wilderness, open to the embankment foot –
our joint dividing wall a crumbled wreck –
with pincer movement towards the licensed herbs
and blameless flowers our landlord has permitted...
where having shortly pitched their silk pavilions
they trumpet victory in all directions.

"If you were half a man you'd weed that garden,"
my conscience hectors me until I rise
to put down their triumphal provocation.
Tough strings are tangled up with flowers and bushes
but pulled in handfuls come at last unravelled
with all the incandescent bells attached
that find a common grave inside the bin.

Recovering from the punitive excursion,
sweaty and scratched and raw with nettle-stings,
I see the enemy, still undefeated,
mock my discomfort through the kitchen window.

A glowing tapestry of white on green
proclaims the lords of life still rampant there.

Time, Please

Time in his kitchen chops and sprinkles dates,
blends past with present, folds in what's to come.
See flints and forests and tectonic plates
deform like pastry underneath his thumb!
His recipes are altered every day:
African warthog, bird of paradise...
Though nothing's lost and nothing's thrown away,
he never serves the same confection twice.

Spiced for the oven, spaced out row on row,
gingerbread man can't contemplate defeat.
spread limbs protesting, mouth an open O
(the picture flawed, the puzzle incomplete,
the seed unspent, the work not finished yet)
he cries for time. And Time is what he'll get.

The Parcel

"What's this? *Notorious thief and fornicator*
who pounces first and asks permission later...
Or this? *Revered and honoured. Rich in years.*
Fulfilled and fruitful. Worth a nation's tears..."

said Peter in the Quartermaster's stores,
peering through pebble specs. "No, this one's yours:

One of the awkward squad. A fool who waits
for half a lifetime doing work he hates.
Too much the gentleman for depth of passion.
Clerk to lost causes. Always out of fashion."

He slapped the parcel, stood there arms akimbo
while I deciphered: *Destination Limbo.*

Fragments Overheard at Northampton Asylum

1

Here's an unfortunate creature, ladies and gentlemen,
driven insane by an aristocratic muse
that liked a bit of rough trade now and then.
Be careful where you step in your polished shoes.

2

You sir, having been cosseted for a while,
displayed a most ungentlemanly passion
when those with taste grew tired of the peasant style
and you couldn't keep up with the caravan of fashion.

3

Having scrabbled for immortality all your life,
even in the dirt of the rubbish heap they flung you on,
can you feel it under black fingernails like a knife
as you slide down the long slope to oblivion?

Three Poems for Jane

1. Magnum Opus

Our mother's voice along the line,
abrupt and inarticulate ("*Jane's in hospital*")
unlocks remorse for months of unpaid visits,
unwritten letters, unmade telephone calls
in simulation of the guilt she's known
since the unexpected last of her four children
arrived blue-lipped and breathless,
bearing a magnum opus of a disease.

> FALLOT'S TETRALOGY *(according to Dorland)*
> *is a combination of congenital cardiac defects*
> *consisting of (1) pulmonary stenosis,*
> *(2) interventricular septal defect,*
> *(3) dextroposition of the aorta*
> *so that it overrides the interventricular septum*
> *and receives venous as well as arterial blood*
> *and (4) right ventricular hypertrophy.*

In and out of hospital all her life,
schooled with the lame, the backward and misshapen
but a party animal, a boon companion,
a skinhead girl marrying into twins,
she has broken every record for survival
and still keeps coming back, each time less far,
to a shrinking radius of independence –
inside the front door a folding wheelchair;
close to her hand a cylinder of oxygen.

> *PULMONARY STENOSIS: a narrowing of the opening*
> *between the pulmonary artery and the right ventricle.*

A family unskilled at communication,
we meet as strangers in a foreign country
where having ordered meals and asked directions
we have exhausted our philosophy,
the television on in every room
levelling out the gaps in conversation
as awkward siblings, carapaced like crabs,
half-conscious of the dynamite and bullets
that Quartermaine explodes across the screen,
dance tipclaw sideways through the killing fields.

> OVERRIDING AORTA: *a congenital anomaly*
> *occurring in the Tetralogy of Fallot,*
> *in which the aorta is displaced to the right*
> *so that it appears to arise from both ventricles*
> *and straddles the ventricular septal defect.*

Once at Christmas she and I and her husband
sat getting steadily drunker on neat whisky
until she dragged us down to her armchair
head to head in a clumsy triple embrace,
whispering through malt tears: "Look after each other."

The medical definitions are based on those in Dorland's Illustrated Medical Dictionary, 27th Edition, 1988, (pages 108, 1580, 1701),

Their permission to quote is gratefully acknowledged.

2. Heart-Lung Transplant

About suffering they were never wrong,
The Old Masters: how well they understood
Its human position, how it takes place
While someone else is eating or opening a window
or just walking dully along.
Auden, Musée des Beaux Arts

In the operation your kidneys went to sleep
and now the blood slides through transparent tubes
in and out of a stainless steel drum,
your mouth clamped open on the ventilator,
cheeks pinched in by the ribbon securing it,
eyes half-lidded with the whites staring.

Come again
from where you've gone...

out of a hot present that's mostly pain,
an egoless near-vegetable existence
where only the automatic nervous system
(left to its own devices without an officer
and stumbling with its captive heart and lungs)
retreats blindly across No Man's Land...

(I sip my drink and read a magazine
as memory flickers like a fruit machine.
Synaptic circuits flash in quick succession
on Greed, Discomfort, Vanity, Aggression
and other regulars that line the bar.
Now Fear and Pity swell my repertoire
and while the standard set keeps cycling through
these hover on the square that signals You)

the lungs still showing evidence of rejection
but the heart beating as if born into its body,
you come awake again, dazed by the shock,
bewildered by the gap from brain to voice
and the obstruction in the throat, you claw
like a trapped wolf at the tracheotomy tube...

Come again
from where you've gone...

having no place to stay – but keep your footing
across the wilderness of forking paths
doubling back to meet each other. Avoid
the easy slope to the unremembering water.
Make for the path that climbs.

3. What's Left

Responding to your mother's voice
you pulled your tongue in, forced a smile
but couldn't will your way towards
a road still climbing mile on mile

and so we left for what life's left,
with no salute or shot or shout
to mark the unrecognised frontier
from world-with-you to world-without:

without the set of mouth and chin
defiantly alive and blue,
the mobile hands and smile and shrug
that wouldn't let it get to you

or play the willing victim's game;
you held your cards close, hid your fears,
sarcastic, vulnerable and brave,
for twice your allocated years.

The operation failed at last
and while we power ahead, you spin
spreadeagled on the black of space,
an astronaut whose lifeline's gone.

Because I couldn't hold the thought
that all those hopes and fears were dead,
I made a virtual life-support
and carried you inside my head

through sodden February hills
down ways your wheelchair's never been;
I pointed you to where through sticks
buds pushed their blind way, moist and green;

but near a huge decaying church
across the concrete underpass
while lorries groaned through neon dusk,
I felt you settle into place

in your familiar territory
of muddy, fingermarked belief,
to which I turned in sceptic prayer,
incontinent with unshed grief

as when unsteady fingers move
the drip-tray brimming from the fridge;
each jog or stumble starts a wave
that slops across its shallow edge.

Unfinished Business

The two of us conversing at the corner,
you summer-dressed against the handlebars
of an unstylish wicker-panniered bike,
recalled how childhood rituals of goodnight
had over and over lengthened family bedtimes,
tying loose ends in case of sudden death,

but in the event achieved no valediction
or else a botched one, tetchy or detached;
and so I stood irresolute while you
mounted the pedals on a casual cue
and went unceremoniously off....
Uncertain what acknowledgement was needed,

I stood and watched you on your way until
some stimulus that stirred a shallow sleep
ejected me, but lodged your after-image,
as limber as in life you never were –
uncalled to as you dwindled towards the turn
and disappeared, with heart and lungs entire.

Mother and Son

The past is packed, the door ajar.
Time yawns and fidgets, eyes his coat
and, like a guest who'll soon be gone,
significantly clears his throat.

So little left before we part –
I search myself for something more
than pleasantries to ease the heart
of this hurt child of eighty-four.

But pleasantries might serve our turn
instead of letting speech congeal,
if either one of us could find
fit formulae for what we feel.

Genetic substance, copied style
conspire, constrict. What we two say
through thickets of inhibitings
and interdicts must find its way –

in hot unhealing grief that crowds
through the resistant throat – or terse
flat sentences we fumble for
like tokens from a clip-lipped purse.

But if in this transaction both
exchange the intentions in what's said,
then such base coinage may suffice
to furnish one day's salt and bread.

Come Back

for my brother

1

You hated fuss,
didn't want our concern,
didn't want to be seen
bald, bloated, dribbling,

clutched the fear and pain
tight to its own house
and we were filtered in
by distant bulletins,

you having laid down how
your wife stood dragon-guard
over the poisoned hoard.
No one can help you now.

2

The complacent heart
has not heard yet –

programmed to trace
the sudden swing right
into that steep street
to see your silhouette
ripple across the glass:

prohibited exchange
bloodbound or spirit-strange;
what passes for a soul,
cold, selfish, shallow,
must settle to its role;

grief is late and slow
to grasp or let me go.

3

Come in dreams
of argument
where contradiction
is of less moment
than engagement;

come in nightmares
of ward-sedated
self sucked away
letting us say
you went without pain.

Come to me any way.

Polyp

1. Enema

Lie on your side, please, with your knees drawn up.
I'm going to administer the enema through this tube,
but first I have to insert a finger to check
there's no obstruction. Please relax. That's good.
Here is the tube. Let me know if you feel discomfort.
OK, that's finished. Now I'm about to withdraw it.
Remain in the same position for five minutes,
or until you feel a powerful urge to go.
The toilets are just opposite.

2. Flexible Sigmoidoscopy

And now another personal violation,
in the same submission posture before an image
that lurches in cinéma-verité down a tunnel
of garish tangerine,
to monitor a self I haven't seen.

Yes, there it is. It's quite a little monster.
We're going to have to cut it out in pieces.

The silver blade goes in and out of shot.

Open. Now close. Open again. Now close.

Something inside has set my teeth on edge
like a fingernail on mortar – not quite pain
but an electric buzz, a scything whisper.
Memory stores the images away
and my attached labelling equipment
begins to shape and generate these words.

That's about half. I'll make another appointment
to finish it. It's probably benign,
but these things can turn cancerous if left.
We'll know for sure after the biopsy.

3. Rectal Washout

What I have to do, my love, is push this tube
up your rectum and pour about a litre of water in
through a funnel. It's going to feel a bit
strange and uncomfortable.
Let me know if it gets too much. That's wonderful, my sweet.
Now I'm removing the tube and I want you to
swing your legs over
and ease yourself off the bed on to this commode.
As soon as you're ready, let it all out and use
the toilet paper, but put it in this bag afterwards.

It hasn't come out, my darling, so I'm afraid
we'll have to go through it again. This time, wriggle your hips
from side to side and wait five minutes on the commode
before letting go.

Yippety-doo! I see polyp

4. Waiting for the Biopsy

According to a theory on the edge
where physics merges into metaphysics
a quantum level indeterminacy
entails a bifurcation of the universe,
invisible layers peeling off each second,
including those my uninvited guest
was absent from. An unmarked road's been taken
and selves diminish down divergent routes
towards their unseen outcomes
while I wait.

Lares

They wheeled me here to find it face to face –
the operation scheduled for today,
this afternoon, this hour, and in this place –
the thing from which I'd turned all thought away.

While images were scrambling in commotion,
as Catholics might call some saint or other
in need, or superstition, or devotion,
I summoned up a sister and a brother.

A prick. A tickling slide. My arm went colder
as, from the cannula they'd piped it through,
the anaesthetic spread towards my shoulder.
The ceiling turned an incandescent blue...

and that was all, till daylight was renewed
in the recovery ward – where, for a time,
I lay abandoned in blank gratitude
as if I had been pardoned of a crime,

except that when the thought returned of Jane
and Tony, who had not, like me, got off
with nothing but a caution and some pain,
a shallow sob exploded like a cough.

The Dark Lady's Reply

You've crafted spells to store me safe from Time
in syllables you'll trade for my caress,
but all that's represented in your rhyme
is my complexion and my fickleness.
Though stock of yours may dig with deeper root
to blossom down the centuries in words,
we light dark girls are wild like autumn fruit:
our immortality is for the birds.

Only by fair exchange can looks beguile.
What unborn fingertips will find my face?
Who'll recognise the way I stretch and smile?
Your gilded frame encloses empty space.
Not brass nor stone nor earth nor boundless sea
can make you keep your promises to me.

Winding Up

After the genital sneeze,
microscopic jostling along the tunnel.
First home snapped the lock behind.
Here we were none of us losers.

The pulsed spawn
of cell division and multiplication
focuses (finned, footed, facial)
with each jerk.

Suddenly blood is racing.
Heart's bud
clenches in spasms.
This fit will stop only once.

Heart knows what's what.
Gulping and squeezing the bright blood,
even in sleep and meditation
his thrash will shake the bed.

Statues

We move to music. When the music ceases
we freeze in postures squalid or sublime –
in time and taste and keeping, or in pieces,
in contradiction, casuistry and crime.

Expedients link to lock our definitions,
and habits we were just about to break
identify us still in fixed positions
anticipating turns we'll never take,

with table overturned and session ended
and system crashed without a chance to save,
all bets wiped out, deliveries suspended,
contrivances to face the impending wave
all smothered in the silt of circumstance.

But now there's music playing. Shall we dance?

Unplugged

I have unplugged myself,
hammered my square peg
into a hollow haven

islanded in alien land
that all lanes lead from –
a slow stone flow

as walls sag uncorseted
thickening towards flagstones
centuries have hollowed

and bursts of lichen
print pale ripples
along a knuckled path

where I watch wagtails strut
up the steep field of thatch
that has become our horizon.

No Through Way

When Eve – as cell – explored simple division,
no crack reporter and no television
crew was on hand to catch the quantum leap,
no pundit to extrapolate the steep
curve of her learning: how to colonise,
attack, ingest, secrete and specialise
in nerve or backbone, liver, heart or brain,
then to divide and multiply again.

Along a protean line the baton passed
a hundred million times, but I'm the last.
Now all the long division left will be
inside the rearguard actions inside me
of social cells in complex interplay,
benign or rogue, controlled or runaway –
before the tree discards its barren shoot
and evolution takes a different route.

Town Squirrel

Acrobat and ballet dancer:
ripples in a flying carpet
wave on wave along the walltop,
fakir-like with perfect judgement
even where an iron railing
pricks its line of bristling spearpoints.

Undulant between the axes
of a horizontal surface
and the force of gravitation,
leaves a track that hangs imprinted
fading like the after-image
of a firestick waved in darkness.

Bat

As the sun draws blinds and walks away
the house-lights dim from yellow to grey
and flighty featherweights floating by
like retina spots against the sky
are culled from the breeze by something quicker
with a savage discontinuous flicker.

You sometimes see it and sometimes not,
a fault in the air, a flying blot,
an absence winging from wall to wall
and you ask, was there anything there at all,
while softly through the occluded light
flits for an hour in black and white
from daytime coffin of cave or cellar
this airborne mouse with skin umbrella.

Distant Flight

Skimming the roofs
in sidelong sun
this morning flock
beats wings as one.

A racing crew
with downbeat bright
as feathers catch
the level light,

an upward stroke
that shows its edge
and then the shadowed
underfledge,

it moves as if
a single mind
controls a shutter
or a blind.

A nebulous
or stippled eye
blinks evenly
across the sky.

Flightpaths

Inhabitants of autumn sky –
two planes distinct with wings and tails,
two more diminished into dots
that drag diverging vapour trails

and one that labours overhead,
its underside exposed to view
with every feature needle-sharp,
set off against ceramic blue –

and while their flightpaths radiate
it brings a little shock to see
a silhouette on ragged wings
home in towards a ragged tree.

Encounter

Butterfly caught in the wiper blade
up against a glass barrier
travelling at 70 mph: was it struggling
to escape, or just riffling in the airstream?
Easing first on to the hard shoulder,
ruefully I offered a finger
for it to grip, and prised it
loose from the rubber and steel trap.
Yellow-white wings seemed whole, but

examination of its mantis profile
now revealed a kink in the abdomen.
Could it fly? No, it spiralled
out of control and crawled
under a wheel. Guessing it
needed shelter I placed it in the long grass where,
trapped, it moved feeble wings.
Even now, I feel cold between the shoulder-blades,
remembering how hard I stamped it into the ground.

Blackbird

Speaking in tongues
with charismatic élan

he interrogates silence
and with grave courtesy weighs each response

or with another at the edge of hearing
duels like a jazz maestro:

against sky on roof-ridge a flickering throat
blows Easy Street for solo clarinet,

old onomatopoeic riffs articulated
in fire-new improvisation:

chirrup trill tirra-lirra
cherrypick cherrypick scorch it scorch it scorch it...

Resistance

As the aesthetics of limbo
polarise the division
between hardliners and fuzzies,

gangs of louche impressionists
spill from café to café,
bullying the bespectacled

to see myopically bare
the play of light on water,
to map movement in air,

moments of transformation;
while underground hardliners,
defiantly horn-rimmed,

cluster in stone cellars
(always with one ear cocked for
the arrival of the fuzz)

to study the banned works
of Brueghel, Blake, Dürer.
Their preferred art is sculpture.

What turns them on is
the uncompromising clarity
of lines, definitions, boundaries,

things becoming themselves
(each with its weight and outline)
by excluding other things;

seeing how in the heavens
where all forms are allowed,
one cloud resembles nothing
so much as another cloud.

Pussycat

for David Bircumshaw

Pussycat, Pussycat, Where have you been?
I've been back to Brum to examine the scene.

Pussycat, Pussycat, what did you there?
I girded my loins and I let down my hair.

Pussycat, Pussycat, What's that you've got?
I've packed a quart poem inside a pint pot.

Pussycat, Pussycat, surely you joke!
To me it resembles a pig in a poke,
a windowless cellar you've filled up with coal,
that beckons me balefully like a black hole.

Behind its horizon dimensions unfold
where light marries darkness and flame feeds on cold.
I could sell you a key to unfasten the locks
and make it spring out like a jack-in-the-box.
but just for this evening it's yours for a song.
With such a fine offer you can't go far wrong.

Anti-Sestina

Won't someone help me? I'm trapped inside a sestina,
condemned like K for a crime I never committed,
sentenced by an inexorable system
to serve without remission seven stanzas –
to watch the same six words keep reappearing
in an exercise yard of banal repetition.

What is the point of so much repetition?
Is there a sillier form than this sestina,
this six-card shuffle and deal, this reappearing
of the six bare words to which I was first committed
with no significant progress for six more stanzas?
I'd like to shoot whoever thought up this system!

It feels like a sort of Groundhog Day, a system
by which all dawns are doomed to repetition
in only superficially different stanzas.
I pray to the evil demiurge *Sestina* –
Let me not be eternally committed
to the selfsame six delinquents reappearing!

But speak of the devil and here comes "reappearing"
striking its hour as if in some intricate system
devised by a mad horologist committed
to clockwork manikins made for repetition
until the pointless programming of the sestina
has slackened all the spring in its tedious stanzas!

How am I going to fill two more of these stanzas?
If this same gibberish keeps on reappearing
I'll soon be a blubbering victim of Sestina,
a casualty defeated by the system.
O Chinese water torture of repetition!
Bring on the straitjacket. Let me please be committed!

But no such easy escape. Since I committed
myself to do it, I'll finish all the stanzas,
keep on flushing away till each repetition
has been repeated and what keeps reappearing
has been evacuated from the system.
And so I bid farewell to this sestina!

Primal crimes are committed that keep reappearing.
Mutant stanzas evolve an ecosystem.
Out of such repetition grows a sestina.

Art

from the French of Théophile Gautier

Those media work best
that are with greatest stress
  processed:
bronze, marble, enamel, verse.

Bondage is form's abuse;
but to walk even-paced
  the Muse
wears buskins tightly-laced,

while fashionable shops,
fitting all feet, stock mostly
  flipflops
that clack while flapping empty.

Don't mess about with clay –
stuff you can knead by thumb
  in play
when images won't come.

In the resistant stone
of Paros or Carrara
  it's known
that the cut lines are purer.

And take from Syracuse
such bronze as can be made
  to expose
your sharp incisive blade.

With a judicious hand
this vein of agate trace,
  and find
the god Apollo's face.

Avoid what's thin and wet.
Let the uncertain haze
  be set
in hard enamel glaze.

Give siren, mermaid, whale
their sinuosity
  of tail –
heraldic bestiary –

and in the triple lobe
with Christ and Mary place
  a globe
surmounted by a cross.

Art's all that we can trust
for immortality:
  a bust
will outlast a city,

and one austere medal
found by a labourer
  in soil
restores an emperor.

Verses are sovereign
and they, though gods may pass,
  remain
more durable than brass.

Let chisel, mallet, file
splinter and flake and knock –
  to seal
dreams in the rigid block.

Productivity

a response to Gautier

No one sweats at the block like that,
grinding stone to a fleshlike sheen.
Labour-intensive art's old hat.
Why not do it in plasticine?

The Rules

1. The Players

i. According to context, the term *poem* may refer to (a) the words common to each hand or (b) the hand unique to each player.
ii. *Reader* and *Listener* are distinct players, even when occupying the same body.
iii. There must be at least two players, including the dealer (but see 3.iii).
iv. The dealer may (and initially must) occupy the same body as one of the other players.
v. If a player leaves and returns to a game, the hand shall be deemed to be a new hand (see 2ii). No poem steps into the same reader twice.

2. The Words

i. The dealt words are common to all players.
ii. Each player also has up to five senses and a history, which may include a presence at previous deals.
iii. Certain combinations of the above may control breath, pulse, hair, and skin.

3. The Deal

i. The dealer shuffles and deals the words until it is deemed that any further deal would produce an inferior hand.
ii. From this point on, the dealer has no automatic privilege over other players.
iii. A dealer who leaves the table shall nevertheless be deemed to be a player for the purposes of rule 1.iii.
iv. The game continues until the words are exhausted and/or there are no players physically present at the table.

Kind Ghost

Afford a beggar halt and blind
what loving-kindness you can find
  to distribute in alms from your
sufficiency – and I'll be kind

when, clustering on the edge of thought,
not kind ghosts but another sort
  display unhealed in open palm
stigmata from your edged retort,

or those whose life you couldn't face,
but held back from a willed embrace,
  besiege your bed at break of dawn
and mock your flesh with empty space.

To a Piece of Software

My hatred of you increments in ways
that integers can't count nor words express.
A CPU would take ten thousand days
to calculate your bloodymindedness:

those secret files to which I've lost the keys;
the way you take *exception* on no basis
to kindly meant remarks; the way you freeze
in unresponsive catatonic stasis,
or curtly quit with '*unexpected error*';
the ticklishness that's triggered by a mouse;
the *general protective* paranoia
that drives you in a huff out of the house.

Let's face it son, you're tacky through and through!
I almost wish I hadn't written you.

Two Voices

There are two voices tempting you.
One tells you what you ought to do –
at which the other screams and cries
with stamping feet and screwed-up eyes.

One carves commandments into stone.
His hard uncompromising tone
demands obedience to the letter.
The other's sure that he knows better.

For one's a slave to tongue and groin
and wastes his master's hard-won coin
on drink and drabs and rolling dice
while the other groans for sacrifice.

There is no reconciling these,
for one is chalk to the other's cheese,
and yet the ill-assorted pair
travel together everywhere.

Embraced like drunks, they lurch and swing
as one asserts that anything
worth doing is worth doing well
and the other's code is *What the hell!*

Sweet Charity

A poetry society found that the Council grant which it thought it had been getting had actually come from the pocket of the Treasurer, who had forgotten to post the application and had been too embarrassed to tell the Committee. Unfortunately, they had allowed the Council logo to appear on their literature.

Huffily, stuffily Charity Camberley
hoarded her umbrage and honed her disdain,
hearing the Puddlecombe Poetry Circle
had got itself into a pickle again.

Pickily, pettily Charity chided:
"Someone should teach you a lesson this time.
Officers have to protect Council Property.
Logo abuse is a serious crime:

"I smell malpractice and irregularity.
Something's been festering right from the first:
Some individual must have been profiting
out of the bounty we haven't disbursed."

Whisking support like a carpet from under them,
what a cacophony Charity stirred –
poets two-fingering Charity's homilies,
taking the mickey and giving the bird!

Undaunted Charity, fierce as a valkyrie,
laid down the law with a frown on her face:
"Now you'll think twice before taking our name in vain.
Poets have got to be put in their place.

"No one will dare to be caught in your company:
Arts in the Sticks are our supplicants too.
Pipers must play what's permitted by paymasters.
So long then, suckers...and so much for you."

Sympathetic Magic

1

Conceive a clear enclosure where, alone,
light spills and settles over whitewashed stone
and clings to porcelain like clotted cream.
Simplicity and space. It's good to dream.
Consider now a room unswept, unaired,
a bed that's seldom made and seldom shared –
emerging from the quilt the blank white faces
of pillows half-undressed from pillowcases.
Another weekend waits for fumbling hands
to unwrap promises and reprimands,
while rituals of rising and ablution
postpone inevitable retribution.

2

By now the post has generated more
thick sheaves of junk to bin and guilt to store.
Cue in the background tape of classic blues.
The long late breakfast and the morning's news
digest a day already past its prime.
So many things to do. So little time.
A word-infested world, with no escape
from these parameters that fix its shape.
And when the room is packed too tight to think,
uncleanly carpeted with printer's ink,
what hands are these that prickle in my hair?
What presses down the ceiling, drains the air?

3

Our primitive precursors fashioned means
of filtering their world through magic screens –
in masks and cloaks compelled the totem prey;
lit fires that helped the sun to rise next day;
wore talismans to blind the evil eye
and muttered charms before they rolled a die.
Beset by gibbering mouths on every side
and overrun by chaos, I can hide
in hollow artefacts contrived from spells,
with holes for eyes and lips like trumpet bells,
whose glittering metal masks a crumpled face
dreaming about simplicity and space.

Not Marble...

...More like shaping a hedge.
What's carved in language from day one
loses proportion, blurs detail
as growing points obscure the edge
that shears precisely clipped.

Soon what the gardener made has gone.
How can a soft growth outlast all
the sand-scoured, surface-stripped
columns, frieze and frontage
of tactile, tough material?

The Poet Bequeaths his Germs

I'd rather be remembered for my style,
my captivating poise, my smouldering look,
my subtle wit, my rare infectious smile –
or else because you've purchased my new book.
But in default of rhetoric to bend
your mind to my mind, imagery to freeze
your blood and make your hair stand up on end,
I can be with you still in my disease.

Inside the lining of your lungs I'll creep
and take possession irresistibly.
My wastes, if not my words, will make you weep.
Awake at night, you will remember me.
My influence will colonise your day,
constrict your throat and take your breath away.

Mask

Torres Strait, Australia, 1877 (Pitt Rivers Museum, Oxford);
used in initiation and funerary ceremonies

Turtle shell
cleaned and scoured
cut to a lattice,
feathers incised
along horizontals.

Two white ovals
with pigment pupils
between which dangles
a cartoon handle
of a nose.

This mask
is rife with mouth.
A gap-grin curls
up to its ears.
Further south
a prim oval's
feathered teeth
reprise the eyes.

On the pendulum neck
a crescent arc
or boat or torque
grins like a shark.
It rattles and clacks
with nutshell-strings
to summon up
sub-
liminal things.

Talents

It isn't what you mean but what you say.
Spades outrank hearts. The deal may not be fair.
There's no disposing love that's locked away.
Disjunctive virtue dissipates in air.
So when the next depression lies in wait,
invest in guilts whose value will accrue.
Effects depend on causes. Your estate
is circumscribed by what you've failed to do.

Don't lift up stones to peer at what's beneath –
fine gestures that allowed conceit to grow
or decent things you did with gritted teeth –
for what the world will measure, even though
your motivation's rotten to the core,
is what you made, not what you made it for.

All Present and Correct

Above Malham Tarn
where the hillside grew steep,
the only things living
were me and the sheep...

Here, hang on a minute,
you speciesist prat,
there was grass growing everywhere –
don't forget that!

and mosses and lichen
and nettles and stuff
and little brown...
Thank you,
but that's quite enough.

Your point is well taken;
your views I respect.
I'll try to rephrase it
in words more correct:

Above Malham Tarn
where the hillside grew steep,
the only large mammals
were me and the sheep...

Excuse me again, squire,
but my teacher reckoned
it was always politer
to put yourself second.

Many thanks for your comment.
I'll take it to heart,
and with that in mind
I'll go back to the start:

Above the grey water
the harsh wind blew free.
The only large mammals
were some sheep and me...

  Now that's a lot better,
  but surely "to be"
  should not take an object?
Yes, yes, I agree:

Above the grey water,
beneath the grey sky,
the only large mammals
were some sheep and I...

Except that the sheep
had all wandered away,
and I'm going too,
so I'll bid you good day.

Air and Earth

The atmosphere in this outlandish place
(enclosed by silhouetted towers and trees)
with endless patience kneads an open space
that folds upon itself in dazed unease,
ripples from end to end as if in pain,
bruises and heals, lets go and starts again.

This weather washing over us in waves
(and readjusting latticeworks of leaves
as the air agitates their empty caves)
indifferently detaches or reprieves.
These seas of serendipity will not
be scooped inside a poem's poor pint pot.

But stake your rhymes out square in solid ground
and stretch your lines between until they sing,
then drape your silken panels all around.
They'll tremble in the wind but not take wing,
though beating up in waves like fields of wheat –
the air is fit for wings, the earth for feet.

Snap

That ancient beech (blown down in last year's storm)
lay horizontal like a giant axle
from which the snapped roots radiated spokes,
the hollow they vacated dense with grass,
and warm bark made a comfortable bench.

Here we could loll at ease and pose for pictures,
five in a row – and not one of us noticed
that two or three roots buried in the soil
were feeding sap towards the other end,
whose branches were still putting out fresh growth
with leaves luxuriating in the sun.

Sodden and Unkind

When I am living in the Midlands
That are sodden and unkind,
I light my lamp in the evening:
My work is left behind;
And the great hills of the South Country
Come back into my mind.

Hilaire Belloc

You've caught us bang to rights, Belloc:
these sneers and snarls confess
what a mean morass of malignant minds,
what a squalidly squelching mess
extends from Leek to Leamington Spa,
from Cannock Chase to Skegness.

You've scanned us through to the soul, Hilaire:
black sheep for mile on mile,
no mapped gradations into grey,
no fat manila file
suggesting 3.5 bags full.
Precision's not your style.

A train excursion once up north
(you were there and back in a day)
was field research for your holding forth
in that magniloquent way
how men's hearts were "set upon the waste fells"
from Hull to Whitley Bay.

On "the great hills of the South Country"
the peasant spits and plods.
I've known a good few sons of the soil
and some were as unkind sods
as ever mauled vowels in Birmingham
to the hiss of connecting rods.

While you're off "walking in the high woods"
we'll pustulate in peace
(miserable marsh-bred misanthropes,
felons and pharisees)
and I'll update my notes on the neighbour's kids
before informing the police.

Encouragement to a Foot Soldier

With Victoriana there's nothing amiss,
so please don't imagine I'm taking the piss.
Pastiche of past taste has abiding appeal:
you cannot conceive how encouraged I feel
to know there is someone respectful enough
of Housman and Kipling and Arthur Hugh Clough
to play variations on their compositions.
We mustn't neglect such poetic traditions.

There's much mileage left in the birds and the bees
and evergreen topics as timeless as these.
Anapaestic tetrameter still has its charms,
like lavender bags and embossed coats of arms
and popular classics on Radio 2.
In the House of the Muse there's a mansion for you
(though its gothic embellishment does seem a waste
and the plasterwork isn't to everyone's taste).

You can entertain visitors there, if you must,
with cucumber sandwiches minus the crust,
with bone-china tea-parties on the three-piece
and erudite fancies from classical Greece
in varying forms and rhetorical modes,
sestets and sestinas and sonnets and odes:
maintaining a measure of civilised grace
while we party on in the rest of the place.

Treadmill

Five days a week and seven hours a day,
assigned to servicing the wealth machine,
you watch the clock and wish your life away.

Incorporated in the great display
of citizens and soldiers, on the scene
five days a week and seven hours a day,

alive at weekends and on holiday,
on autopilot all the waste between,
you watch the clock and wish your life away.

The system knows its needs and you obey
the prompts and pointers on the flickering screen
five days a week and seven hours a day.

They start your actions, script the things you say,
patrol the borderlines of what you mean.
You watch the clock and wish your life away.

Until the boundaries of work and play
are by a change of common heart wiped clean,
five days a week and seven hours a day
you'll watch the clock and wish your life away.

Christmas Turkeys

a dialogue between public and politician

You come across like folks with your Christmas-cracker jokes.
Your forehead's fiercely furrowed with responsible concern.
But we know that underneath you are lying in your teeth
and praying when the music stops it's you for Buggins' turn.

When I started in this game I was keeper of the flame.
Now so far up the greasy pole I've lost all sense of shame.
I've seen the nice guys finish last, and this is my conclusion:
you all give thanks to mountebanks that flatter your illusion.

You know how best to line the nest.
                    You say it's common sense
to get things done for number one.
                    You like your market shady,
with hands in tills and words in ears
                    and scratching backs for pence
through covert links of nods and winks
                    and *Say-no-more-Milady...*

If we are willing whores, then the lusts we serve are yours:
for a penny off the basic rate you're drooling at the jaws –
so beady and astute that you'll kiss my hobnailed boot
when I auction your inheritance and give you half the loot.

You scatter *Brave Tomorrow* and *Bright Dawn*
to turkeys fed on factory-frozen corn.

Yes, we've only to re-heat it. You can have your cake
                    and eat it
and it's Christmas in the battery shed
                    before you know you're born.

The Death of the Ogre

Close to the tree that grows the poisoned fruit,
where scents of ancient murder spice the air,
he crushed old bones beneath his riding boot
and stepped at last into the ogre's lair.

Having blown out the fatuous goblin-light,
spitted the ghoul that wore the angelic face
and slain the demons gibbering left and right,
he'd grown almost familiar with the place.

A single thrust dispatched its bloated lord –
and so the story starts. Debauched with fighting,
he stared out of the window at the broad
fields of the ogre, fertile and inviting.
Corruption temporarily exiled
fills up vacated space. The ogre smiled.

My 9:11

Someone's just flown a plane into the World Trade Center
says a guy in the office
and when I visit the online news site
it's true and I'm half cheering

and a second plane has flown into a second tower,
the site updating minute by minute,

clips of the impact and the windows exploding
                                                            out the other side
coming in pulses and pixels
jerky like Franz Ferdinand's motorcade

and I'm not considering people looking up from their screens
to see a plane flying straight towards them
or those on other floors saying *What was that?*
and being told *Stay where you are! Don't panic!*

and when the newsfeed reports that a tower has fallen
and people have been jumping
I imagine them landing from the first floor and running away
or climbing like beetles out of a fallen tree

until the clips come through of the towers telescoping
down into their own dust
like the evil beauty of a mushroom cloud

and it's days before the reaction comes,
not grief or mourning but simple comprehension
focusing down on people in offices, stairwells, lifts
and outside running in desperation across the open ground.

Autumn Room

This is my autumn room. Observe the blue
dome, how it deepens upward, how the clouds
are always different when they move across it.

The fan is on the lowest setting, enough
to unsettle the pool, cross-hatch the mirrored stems.
One cloud swims out over it like a fish.

Admire this tree, how its few copper leaves
along arthritic branches are supplemented
by thick green moss and grey dishevelled lichen.

The gravel rug creaks underneath your feet
but if you stand quite still you'll hear the bird
that flickers weightlessly from branch to branch
stop to unscroll its king-of-the-castle cry.

Presence

Romans inherited a manual and digital
mathematics of gesture: one, two, three
raised fingers; five in a spread palm's wedge
meaningful to a foreigner or deaf-mute;
eighteen a double handful, a handful and three;
the common language of a marketplace
where pedlars squatted in the dust beside their cloths
in walking distance of farms and backstreet workshops.
Alien dialects and complexions haggled
currencies tangible to teeth and palms.

Even the elements took things personally:
wind whipped and caressed; the sky's battery
discharged itself with unpredictable power
on field and fold and flesh. Presence was everywhere
angry and gluttonous, to be placated
by ritual wastage and votive offering
accompanied by proper invocation
(neglect of which might summon plague or lightning
or blight a crop whose ripening in most years
just filled the gap between satiety and famine).

We have channelled lightning and set rules for weather:
traffickers elevated to their office
transact, negotiate and represent
by disembodied voice and keyed return
in markets where there is nothing to bite or smell
as power swells up in tiers of abstracted profit,
whipping typhoons not seasonal or material
but circling through collective whim and hysteria,
smashing down trees with bolts of electricity,
capricious, heartless, targeting by numbers.

Border

The Future is a country
to which travel is permitted
on a cheap one-way ticket.

Behind explored edges
the interior remains
a cartographer's white hole

where visitors are excluded
and communication with natives
is uncertain and unreciprocated,

though some spend time
signalling into the mist
with megaphone and semaphore,

even their smalltalk
edited for correctness
in case spies are about.

Refugees, once processed,
inhabit makeshift shelters
in camps along the border,

clutching temporary visas,
knowing that they can never
return to where they were born

yet fearing repatriation;
they clamour for reports
on the shifting balance of power

as the frontier retreats and retreats
before the constant pressure
for *lebensraum* by History

(the totalitarian state
that keeps its chief citizens
under constant surveillance

and allows the population
only a single response
to each situation).

In Memory of John Thomas

In
Mem y
O
JOHN T AS
SON OF THOMAS AH THOMAS
OF HEPTONST DIED FEB 22ND
1875 AGEI 8 YEARS
ALSO OF THOMAS THOMAS HIS
FATHER, WHO DIED JULY 23RD 1875
AGED 61 YEARS.
In the midst of life we are in death.
ALSO OF SARAH, RELICT OF THE SAID
THOMAS THOMAS, WHO DIED OCTR 30
1888, AGED 72 YEARS.
ALSO OF HARRIET THOMAS,
DAUGHTER OF THE ABOVE, WHO DIED
AUGT 28TH 191 AGED 56 YEARS.
"AT REST."

Frost, or a like disintegrating hand,
having removed a lozenge from the surface
of this memorial, sets its chisel in
under the edges of the open wound
to prise away the skin in crumbling flaps.
Lower, and to the left, a jagged line
marks the emergence of another blister
and Harriet's end is in dilapidation.

I am perhaps the last to read the inscription
and soon shall have no power to reconstruct it
so, to perform a service for a stranger,
I dig a scrap of paper from my pocket
and scribble down the epitaph in pencil
as if to make finality less final.

Take 2

If I could engineer a second go
inside some previous self – fingers and thumbs
unfumbling this time, steering him just so
to step the sweetest way and steal the plums –

I'd squint astutely through his visored skull,
a potent manikin who knows the score,
who's checked the chief scenarios in full
and found what combination works what door.

But while I contemplate this guiding role,
another self from somewhere down the line,
who waits to ease me out and take control,
is grimacing at new mistakes of mine.

Through soundproof screens each future mouths advice,
but presents never get presented twice.

Alternatives

A chance mutation in a sewer
may replicate and so repeat
that from the press of things impure
the pavement cracks beneath our feet,

and accidental angels walk
unrecognised from place to place
upon polluted territory
scattering surreptitious grace.

We improvise successive selves
as, incident by incident,
alternatives like fans of cards
exfoliate from each event

where with impassive protocol
the icy gambler in the shades
deals evenly the two of clubs,
the joker or the queen of spades.

Sun

All the shadow sight could find
sickened in that caustic glare.
I've stared until I'm almost blind.
Such clarity pervades the air,
which way I turn the sun is there
but still the shadow turns behind.

Genes

I'm stuck with Dad's myopic squint
and Grandpa's stilted stride.
This mother's son sings out of tune.
Time flows but genes abide.

The Real World

Although you represent what I believe
I can't vote for you because you are not credible.

I will vote for what I don't believe
for fear my vote may be wasted.

The candidate I will vote for
secretly believes as I do

but dares not say so
for fear of losing my vote.

Unlike you,
he and I live in the real world.

Fairy Tale

Square-gaping rage:
the flat slam of his axe.

The freezing steel
of the Queen's needle.

Whispering trickster:
his spittle sticks to the skin.

Moon, open-mouthed
in blown robes.

Under autumn's mulch
the plump grubs burrow.

The Bad Fairy at the Christening

You don't need second sight to know the future.
It isn't *what*, but *when* and *where* and *how*
that circumstances may permit to differ.
I prophesy the bare essentials now:

the Prince and Princess didn't get together;
the Emperor was not disposed to laughter;
the knight in armour didn't kill the dragon;
they didn't all live happy ever after.

Life stretches out its unlit road to nowhere.
You've taken on a bet you cannot win.
The years line up like footpads with shillelaghs,
and one of them is sure to do you in.

Better to travel in hope than to arrive
at journey's end. No one gets out alive.

Optimist

Rain fell yesterday in the East Midlands
to a depth of three inches
and – although the measuring system
is undoubtedly more sophisticated
than my imagined tin on the roof
of the local weather station –
I assume three inches to mean
the same three inches
in car parks and shopping precincts
as in meadows and plant nurseries.

Extrapolating statistically, therefore,
from your belief
that for every drop of rain that falls
a flower grows
and allowing, for the sake of argument,
an average raindrop
to be a quarter of an inch in diameter,
I foresee in the most favourable conditions
seed souls stacked and circling like jumbo jets,
rootlets extended,

and not only fierce jostling
between root systems,
but every shoot
having to survive on a single drop of water,
the next one being allocated
to a different flower:

a Darwinian mêlée
more likely to produce
cacti than chrysanthemums.

In Camera

Nomadic lives migrate from day to day.
The wind unwinds our tracks across the sand.
Experience gets chalked up and wiped away
unless some lineaments are fixed by hand
in pigment or in ink – for which we pay
with hours of work for every image scanned –
or take machinery that has the trick
of mummifying moments in a click.

Possess your cake or eat it crumb by crumb,
defining grain and fruit and aftertaste.
Photographers like lepidopterists come
with killing jars, determined not to waste
this colonnade, that atmospheric slum.
They want them packaged, portable and placed –
but swimming through a second's not the same
as squinting at it sliced inside a frame.

And unsophisticated cultures knew
photography could steal away a soul.
Each candid snapshot filches part of you
that your self-definition can't control:
a keyhole cameo, a mole's-eye view,
a puzzle building in towards its hole
with pieces that aspire to fill the heart
whose emptiness still holds their frame apart.

Advice to Poets

Be patient with the one that calls
when brick by brick you've built your walls.
His muscles may has gone to waste
but he still has exquisite taste.
Although not fit to clear hard ground,
he'll shift your furniture around
and lisp while lounging in the shade
of the strong structure you have made:
"Those flowers and curtains clash, my dear,
and you don't need that lamp in here."

Mistrust the military style
encouraging his rank and file
with manly clasp and shoulder clap –
"Jolly good show, well done old chap!" –
such tokens as the service pays
in standard-issue words of praise.
His firm adjustment of your tie
may interrupt your air-supply,
and fumblings with a ribbon-pin
through khaki folds can find your skin.

Endure the analytic mind,
the ferret face more keen than kind
who'll subject to a third degree
the images in stanza three,
putting their honesty in doubt
until they've turned their pockets out,
then deign at last to let you pass
certificated second class
and stamp his qualified consent –
obliterating what you meant.

A Poem Prays for Survival

When first the Muse's careless spawn
(if not aborted or still-born)
sets out towards your fertile mind,
a predator swims close behind
(oblivion-mouthed, unfeeling, blind)
to gobble up without remorse
what hasn't strength to stay the course:

what's lame and stiff; what's limp and slack
and impotent against attack;
what's bloated, floundering, thick of tongue;
what's pure of heart but fashioned wrong;
and what mutates from verse to prose.

Please let me not be one of those.

Author, Author!

Applause politely ripples – but what beast
accosts us like a spectre at your feast?
What eyes roll greedily and what teeth grin
through what disintegrating rags of skin?
Although the whisper runs that this rude ghost
is our facilitator and our host,
we squirm as if confined in conversation
with some disreputable poor relation.

When you have shuffled off this mortal coil
critics will weigh and measure your life's toil
and the biographer's keen scholarship
will patch those pockets, piece that careless rip,
sew back the label, clean and fold and press
the long-neglected, loosely-lived-in mess
you called your life – and then we'll honour you,
untainted by organic residue.

Letter to a Crowded House

for Anne Kind

I took the victims, over the trench I cut their throats
and the dark blood flowed in – and up out of Erebus they came
flocking towards me now, the ghosts of the dead and gone...
Odyssey, trans Robert Fagles

July the 16th, 1999
Dear Anne,
I hope you're well. Today is fine
and metrical. There'll not be many more
such dates to seed a couplet with before
the shrinks wrap up this shrieking century
and stack the ten decades in history.

You've known more times and territories than most.
Along your head's dark corridors the ghost
of every past self mews for recognition
like Homer's ancestors, whose mute condition
was slaked by blood. You want to give them voice,
build back with words their worlds of sense and choice
that once were yours – and only you are able
to paint the living picture, not the label.
So load your brush and lay the pigment thick,
make lungs lift, lids blink open, pulses tick.

It's tough for me to take my own advice.
Admission to the Muse exacts a price.
Some satisfaction has to be denied,
some sacrifice set down of sloth or pride
before the will and wellspring work together –
and my dry summer seems persistent, whether
for want of inspiration, want of trying
or want of wanting.
All best wishes,
Brian

Summering In

Bees burrow in the blossom's silk interior
as summer's slow tumescence inches towards its climax,
uplifts the sun, stiffens the green stems,
prepares pistil and stamen for interchange of pollen.

Fugitive rape has colonised the verge,
sulphurously alight, loading the ticklish air
that swells the eyelid, stirs the mucous lining
and stimulates the lungs' orgasmic salutation.

Shut every door and barricade the windows
against this frenzy. I must become the season's hermit.
Leave me alone to sieve the summer's lust
with shallow breath. A kiss would be slow suffocation.

Epithalamion

The year's equation cancels out to this
guttered expense, this suffocating gloom
as Proserpine completes the pact with Dis.

What might have been is mating with what is.
While the coarse cloth creeps through the clattering loom
the year's equation cancels out to this

and registers in slow paralysis
each day's descent to meet the impatient groom
as Proserpine completes the pact with Dis,

discovering the dark antithesis
of seed and stamen, foliage and plume.
The year's equation cancels out to this.

And now the Emperor of the Abyss
is pacing with her towards the bridal room
as Proserpine completes the pact with Dis.

The cold god spills his seed of genesis,
dividing and dividing in her womb.
The year's equation cancels out to this
as Proserpine completes the pact with Dis.

How Soon has Time

with apologies to John Milton

How soon has Time, the thief of middle age,
filched on the fly my nine-and-fiftieth year!
Perusing my life's volume, page by page
towards a FINIS no great way from here,
he licks his fingertip with avid tongue,
requiring resolution of this plot,
and scans to where the publisher has slung
his colophon beneath my final dot.

I guess at what the unopened chapters hide -
at what I'd know if I could read myself -
what sharp critiques of intellectual pride
must show before I'm on the archive shelf -
what times of brass must follow those of gold -
with one year left to practise being old.

Boy on a Landing

Down the lit passage an open door,
through the door a dark room,
across the room an uncurtained window.

In this window the dark room doubled,
across the doubled room a door,
a lit passage, a pale-faced child.

What does the child see down the passage,
through the doors of the dark rooms
where a white-haired man enacts his memory?

Printed in the United Kingdom
by Lightning Source UK Ltd.
125308UK00001B/76-153/A